BLACK BRAVE BEAUTIFUL

BLACK BRAVE BEAUTIFUL

The Badass Black Girl's
Coloring Book

M.J. FIEVRE

Mango Publishing
CORAL GABLES

Cover Design: Logan Masterworks
Cover and interior illustrations: Shutterstock
Layout & Design: Logan Masterworks

For permission requests, please contact the publisher at:
Mango Publishing Group
2850 S Douglas Road, 2nd Floor
Coral Gables, FL 33134 USA
info@mango.bz

For special orders, quantity sales, course adoptions and corporate sales, please email the publisher at sales@mango.bz. For trade and wholesale sales, please contact Ingram Publisher Services at customer.service@ingramcontent.com or +1.800.509.4887.

Black Brave Beautiful: The Badass Black Girl's Coloring Book

ISBN: (print) 978-1-64250-529-0, (ebook) 978-1-64250-530-6
BISAC category code YAN024050, YOUNG ADULT NONFICTION / Health & Daily Living / Maturing

Printed in the United States of America

Dear Badass Black Girl,

You are a true warrior who inherited the strength, courage, wisdom, love, and dignity of our ancestors. You stand on their shoulders, carrying a history of triumph. Yes, it is true: you also still carry some of the pain of yesterday's Black heroines—these creators, innovators, and agents of change—and you are faced with the tremendous struggle of the modern girl of color. But make no mistake: you are strong and you can conquer whatever challenges this world hands you.

Your very existence defies history. Never forget those who broke the unjust rules society once used to limit their progress, those who fought hard to get you to this moment, those who gave light so others could find the way through dark times. Because of them, you get to walk into a restaurant through the front door, sit at the front of the bus, and cast a vote for leaders who represent your ideals. Walk in the freedom they secured for your sake. Be proud of your rich skin, and may your hair be a crown that stands tall. Be proud of your deep-rooted culture(s). Be proud of the power of those who came before you, as the strength of generations will propel you forward and carry you through difficulties.

Be fearless. But, as you move through the world, remember: your biggest responsibility is to remain thoughtful, to honor where you come from, and to recognize you didn't simply appear and find your own voice. Alice Walker wrote, "How simple a thing it seems to me that to know ourselves as we are, we must know our mothers' names."

Kenbe (be strong),
MJ

"I have a lot of things to prove to myself. One is that I can live my life fearlessly."

—**Oprah Winfrey**, American media executive, actress, talk show host, television producer, and philanthropist

"You're not obligated to win. You're obligated to keep trying to do the best you can every day."

—**Marian Wright Edelman**, American activist for children's rights

"It was when I realized I needed to stop trying to be somebody else and be myself, I actually started to own, accept, and love what I had."

—**Tracee Ellis Ross**, American actress, model, comedian, director, and television host

"I don't have to be perfect. All I have to do is show up and enjoy the messy, imperfect, and beautiful journey of my life."

—**Kerry Washington**, American actress

"Pledge that you will look in the mirror and find the unique beauty in you."

—**Tyra Banks**, American television personality, producer, businesswoman, actress, author, model, and singer

"What do I love about being Black? Everything. Every. Single. Thing."

—**Susan Kelechi Watson**, actress, *This Is Us*

"Never be afraid to sit awhile and think."

—**Lorraine Hansberry**, Black American playwright and writer

"If you don't like something, change it. If you can't change it, change your attitude."

—**Maya Angelou**, American poet, singer, memoirist, and civil rights activist

"Mistakes are a fact of life. It is the response to the error that counts."

—**Nikki Giovanni**, American poet, writer, commentator, activist, and educator

"It's time for you to move, realizing that the thing you are seeking is also seeking you."

—**Iyanla Vanzant**, American inspirational speaker, lawyer, New Thought spiritual teacher, author, life coach, and television personality

"Yes, I do have a big ego…and I am in love with myself…because if you don't love yourself, how can anybody love you back?"

—**Mel B.**, English singer-songwriter, rapper, producer, model, television personality, and author.

"Whatever we believe about ourselves and our ability comes true for us."

—**Susan L. Taylor**, American editor, writer, and journalist

"Life is very short and what we have to do must be done in the now."

—**Audre Lorde**, American writer, feminist, womanist, librarian, and civil rights activist

"I have learned over the years that when one's mind is made up, this diminishes fear; knowing what must be done does away with fear."

—**Rosa Parks**, American civil rights activist

"There have been so many people who have said to me, 'You can't do that,' but I've had an innate belief that they were wrong. Be unwavering and relentless in your approach."

—**Halle Berry**, American actress

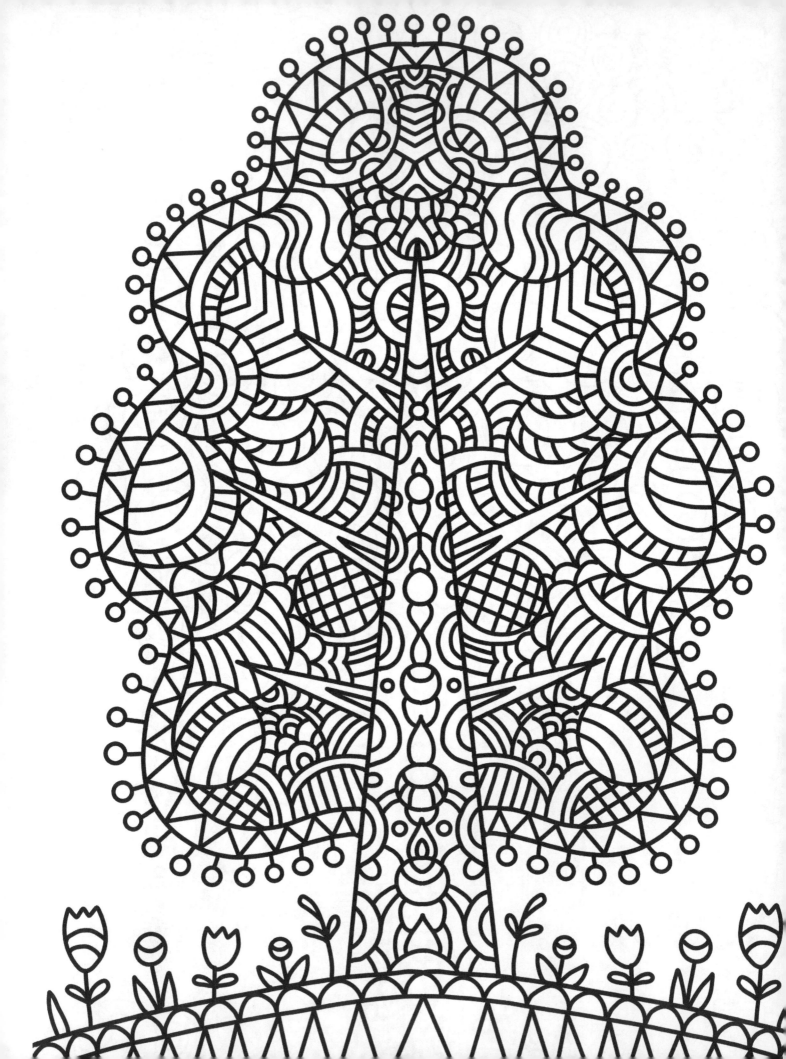

"I always believed that when you follow your heart or your gut, when you really follow the things that feel great to you, you can never lose, because settling is the worst feeling in the world."

—**Rihanna**, Barbadian singer, businesswoman, fashion designer, actress, and philanthropist

"You can't be hesitant about who you are."

—**Viola Davis**, American actress and producer

"Surround yourself with only people who are going to lift you higher."

—**Oprah Winfrey**, American media executive, actress, talk show host, television producer, and philanthropist

"All anyone can hope for is just a tiny bit of love, […] like a drop in a cup if you can get it, or a waterfall, a flood, if you can get that too."

—**Edwidge Danticat**, internationally acclaimed
Haitian American novelist and short story writer

"Everything is worth it. The hard work, the times when you're tired, the times where you're a bit sad; in the end, it's all worth it because it really makes me happy. There's nothing better than loving what you do."

—**Aaliyah**, American singer, actress, and model

"Never underestimate the power of dreams and the influence of the human spirit. We are all the same in this notion: the potential for greatness lives within each of us."

—**Wilma Rudolph**, African American sprinter

"No person is your friend who demands your silence or denies your right to grow."

—**Alice Walker**, American novelist, short story writer, poet, and social activist

"I am a feminist, and what that means to me is much the same as the meaning of the fact that I am Black; it means that I must undertake to love myself and to respect myself as though my very life depends upon **self-love** *and* **self-respect**.*"

—**June Jordan**, Jamaican American poet, essayist, teacher, and activist

"I'm not ashamed of what I am and that I have curves and that I'm thick. I like my body."

—**Alicia Keys**, American musician, singer, and songwriter

"Life was neither something you defended by hiding nor surrendered calmly on other people's terms, but something you lived bravely, out in the open, and that if you had to lose it, you should lose it on your own terms."

—**Edwidge Danticat**, internationally acclaimed Haitian American novelist and short story writer

"Just be honest and true to yourself. If your friends around you love you, they'll wish you the best and want only what's going to make you happy."

—**Meagan Good**, American actress

*"It seems like the entire world has intensely specific opinions on how Black women and girls should be. How we should wear our hair, how we should talk, and the volume at which we should do it. The list goes on: how we should dance, who we should date, what kind of music we should listen to, etc. What I love most about being Black is I've been forced from an early age to confront—and later ignore—all these absurd expectations and live life on my own terms, liberated, with zero F*s left to give."*

—**Nicola Yoon**, author of *Everything, Everything* and *The Sun Is Also a Star*

"Hard days are the best, because that's when champions are made."

—**Gabby Douglas**, American artistic gymnast

"I think us here to wonder, myself. To wonder. To ask. And that in wondering bout the big things and asking bout the big things, you learn about the little ones, almost by accident. But you never know nothing more about the big things than you start out with. The more I wonder, the more I love."

—**Alice Walker**, American novelist and Pulitzer Prize winner, in *The Color Purple*

"Breathe. Let go. And remind yourself that this very moment is the only one you know you have for sure."

—Oprah Winfrey, American media executive, actress, talk show host, television producer, and philanthropist

"In every crisis there is a message. Crises are nature's way of forcing change—breaking down old structures, shaking loose negative habits so that something new and better can take their place."

—**Susan L. Taylor**, American editor, writer, and journalist

"The triumph can't be had without the struggle."

—**Wilma Rudolph**, American sprinter

"I will not have my life narrowed down. I will not bow down to somebody else's whim or to someone else's ignorance. "

—**bell hooks**, American author, professor, feminist, and social activist

"Once you know who you are, you don't have to worry anymore."

—**Nikki Giovanni,** American poet, writer, commentator, activist, and educator

"Give light, and people will find the way."

—**Ella Baker**, African American civil rights and human rights activist

"It's not your job to be likable. It's your job to be yourself. Someone will like you anyway."

—**Chimamanda Ngozi Adichie**, award-winning Nigerian writer

"Sometimes, I feel discriminated against, but it does not make me angry. It merely astonishes me. How can any deny themselves the pleasure of my company? It's beyond me."

—**Zora Neale Hurston**, influential author of African American literature, anthropologist, and filmmaker

"You may encounter many defeats, but you must not be defeated. In fact, it may be necessary to encounter the defeats, so you can know who you are, what you can rise from, how you can still come out of it."

—**Maya Angelou**, American poet, singer, memoirist, and civil rights activist

"We teach girls shame. 'Close your legs. Cover yourself.' We make them feel as though being born female they're already guilty of something. And so, girls grow up to be women who cannot say they have desire. They grow up to be women who silence themselves. They grow up to be women who cannot say what they truly think. And they grow up—and this is the worst thing we do to girls—they grow up to be women who have turned pretense into an art form."

—**Chimamanda Ngozi Adichie**, award-winning Nigerian writer

"Dear Beautiful Black Queens…Never underestimate the beauty of just being YOU. Being your authentic self is powerful, sexy, and courageous!"

—**Stephanie Lahart**, author, poet, youth motivational speaker for at-risk teens, and teen mentor

"I realized that beauty was not a thing that I could acquire or consume, it was something I just had to be."

—Lupita Nyong'o, Kenyan-Mexican actress

"A great figure or physique is nice, but it's self-confidence that makes someone really sexy."

—Vivica A. Fox, American actress, producer, and television host

If life gives you lemons make lemonade

"Dear Exquisite Black Queen…You are original, unique, and exquisite! Embrace your imperfections with confidence and self-love. Your authentic self is your best self! Flaws and all, you're still a rare gem! Black woman, you are phenomenal, please believe that!"

—**Stephanie Lahart**, author, poet, motivational speaker for at-risk teens, and teen mentor

"Just remember the world is not a playground but a schoolroom. Life is not a holiday but an education. One eternal lesson for us all: to teach us how better we should love."

—**Barbara Jordan**, American lawyer, educator, politician, and leader of the civil rights movement

Other books by MJ

Order from:

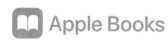

BARNES&NOBLE

B Bookshop

We'd love to hear from you!

Please stay in touch with us and follow us at:

BadassBlackGirl.com

YouTube: Badass Black Girl
Facebook: facebook.com/happyokay.club
Twitter: twitter.com/MJ_Fievre
Instagram: instagram.com/happyokay.club
LinkedIn: linkedin.com/in/m-j-fievre
Pinterest: pinterest.com/mjfievre

About the Author

Born in Port-au-Prince, Haiti, M.J. Fievre moved to the United States in 2002. She currently writes from Miami.

M.J.'s publishing career began as a teenager in Haiti. At nineteen years old, she signed her first book contract with Hachette-Deschamps, in Haiti, for the publication of a Young Adult book titled La Statuette Maléfique. Since then, M.J. has authored nine books in French that are widely read in Europe and the French Antilles. In 2013, One Moore Book released M.J.'s first children's book, *I Am Riding*, written in three languages: English, French, and Haitian Creole. In 2015, Beating Windward Press published M.J.'s memoir, *A Sky the Color of Chaos*, about her childhood in Haiti during the brutal regime of Jean-Bertrand Aristide.

M.J. Fievre is the author of *Happy, Okay? Poems about Anxiety, Depression, Hope, and Survival* (Books & Books Press, 2019) and *Badass Black Girl: Questions, Quotes, and Affirmations for Teens* (Mango Publishing, 2020). She helps others write their way through trauma, build community, and create social change. She works with veterans, disenfranchised youth, cancer patients and survivors, victims of domestic and sexual violence, minorities, the elderly, those with chronic illness or going through transitions, and any underserved population in need of writing as a form of therapy—even if they don't realize that they need writing or therapy.

A longtime educator and frequent keynote speaker (Tufts University, Massachusetts; Howard University, Washington, D.C.; the University of Miami, Florida; and Michael College, Vermont; and a panelist at the Association of Writers & Writing Programs Conference, AWP), M.J. is available for book club meetings, podcast presentations, interviews, and other author events.

Contact MJ @ 954-391-3398 or email happyokay@gmail.com.

Mango Publishing, established in 2014, publishes an eclectic list of books by diverse authors—both new and established voices—on topics ranging from business, personal growth, women's empowerment, LGBTQ studies, health, and spirituality to history, popular culture, time management, decluttering, lifestyle, mental wellness, aging, and sustainable living. We were recently named 2019 and 2020's #1 fastest growing independent publisher by Publishers Weekly. Our success is driven by our main goal, which is to publish high quality books that will entertain readers as well as make a positive difference in their lives.

Our readers are our most important resource; we value your input, suggestions, and ideas. We'd love to hear from you—after all, we are publishing books for you!

Please stay in touch with us and follow us at:

Facebook: Mango Publishing
Twitter: @MangoPublishing
Instagram: @MangoPublishing
LinkedIn: Mango Publishing
Pinterest: Mango Publishing

Sign up for our newsletter at www.mangopublishinggroup.com and receive a free book!

Join us on Mango's journey to reinvent publishing, one book at a time.

CPSIA information can be obtained
at www.ICGtesting.com
Printed in the USA
JSHW022212130221
11896JS00001B/2

9 781642 505290